The Magic of
MINI PIES

*Sweet and Savory
Miniature Pies and Tarts*

The Magic of
MINI PIES

Sweet and Savory
Miniature Pies and Tarts

ABIGAIL R. GEHRING

Skyhorse Publishing

Skyhorse Publishing books may be purchased in bulk at special discounts for sales promotion, corporate gifts, fund-raising, or educational purposes. Special editions can also be created to specifications. For details, contact the Special Sales Department, Skyhorse Publishing, 307 West 36th Street, 11th Floor, New York, NY 10018 or info@skyhorsepublishing.com.

Skyhorse® and Skyhorse Publishing® are registered trademarks of Skyhorse Publishing, Inc.®, a Delaware corporation.

Visit our website at www.skyhorsepublishing.com.

10 9 8

Library of Congress Cataloging-in-Publication Data is available on file.

Print ISBN: 978-1-62087-398-4
eBook ISBN: 978-1-62087-911-5

Printed in China

"We must have a pie. Stress cannot exist in the presence of a pie."

— David Mamet, *Boston Marriage*

{ CONTENTS }

INTRODUCTION

Everyone loves pie—but not everyone loves the same kind of pie. Our family has had Thanksgiving dinners with a dozen different big, beautiful pies, each with one or two slices missing at the end of the day—everyone gets their favorite kind, but it takes days to prepare them all, and the amount of leftovers is downright shameful. Mini pies provide a delicious, sensible, and adorable alternative. They are quick to assemble and bake and allow you to customize your baking to your guests' (or your own) tastes. Make a little apple pie for your aunt, pumpkin for your dad, pecan for the neighbor, and one of each for yourself! (You can always freeze the extras for another day.)

Savory mini pies are perfect for hors d'oeuvres at a gathering or to make ahead of time, freeze, and bring to work for lunch. You can use the recipes in this book to start with and then experiment with your own variations. There are endless varieties of quiches, pizzas, and vegetable or meat pies you can make to satisfy any palate—you can even let kids help create their own individual pies!

What makes a sweeter care package than a few little pies made especially for your loved one? To ship mini fruit or nut pies (don't try shipping very perishable pies, such as meat or cream pies), allow them to cool thoroughly and then wrap each in parchment paper and then plastic wrap or aluminum foil. Freeze the pies overnight. Remove from freezer just before shipping. Find a sturdy cardboard box and cut two thick pieces of Styrofoam that will fit in the bottom of the box. Cut pie-sized holes in the second piece of Styrofoam to place the pies into. Cover with packing peanuts or crumpled newspapers and another layer of foam on top. Ship the pies overnight, if possible, and warn the recipient that something special is coming so the box doesn't end up sitting at the post office or on their back porch for days!

Whether you use a countertop mini pie maker appliance or bake your pies in muffin tins or small pie plates, you may need to experiment with amounts of filling and baking times to get the pies just right. The recipes in this book are geared for four mini pies made in a standard mini pie maker appliance or four pies made in a standard muffin tin.

Happy baking!

—Abigail R. Gehring

{ BAKING MINI PIES }

If you're making mini pies in a countertop appliance, follow the manufacturer's instructions. Start by preheating the pie maker and cutting the dough with the provided dough cutter. Then place the bottom crust rounds over the four cups and fill each a little more than half way. Cover with the top crusts and close the lid to bake for the specified amount of time.

The instructions for your mini pie maker may tell you not to use gravies or custard fillings because too much liquid can make the bottom crusts soggy. I haven't had this problem, but if you do, add more cornstarch or flour to the filling or stick to fruit, nut, or savory fillings that are less liquidy.

The recipes in this book make enough for four mini pies in most standard mini pie maker appliances. If you wind up with extra filling, you can make more pies (most pies can be wrapped in plastic or foil and frozen), freeze the filling for later use, or even eat the filling on its own! If you want to make fewer than four pies, reduce all the ingredients proportionally. Most savory, fruit, and nut pies are fairly forgiving, meaning that if the proportions aren't exact, the pies will most likely still be delicious. Cream and custard

It's easy to make mini pies in muffin tins. The recipes in this book will make four mini pies in regular-sized muffin cups.

pies are less forgiving; if you change the proportions you may end up with a pie that's not the right consistency.

You can also bake mini pies in small pie plates or in muffin tins. Cut the dough in rounds that are large enough to cover the bottom and sides of the tin and to hang over the edge about ½ inch. Press the dough round into the tin. The top rounds can be cut smaller. After you add the filling, place the top crust on and use a fork to seal and crimp the edges. In most cases, you'll need to bake pies in the oven for about 5 to 8 minutes longer than you would in a mini pie maker appliance, though this depends somewhat on the filling and the size of the pies. Pies are done when crusts are golden.

You may need to modify the recipes somewhat to get the right amount of filling, depending on how many pies you're making and what size the tins are. Most of the recipes in this book make about 2 cups of filling.

When using a mini pie maker appliance, press the dough down carefully to make an even indent, and then fill a little more than halfway with pie filling.

MAKING PIECRUST

It seems every baker has her favorite piecrust recipe—some insist a combination of butter and lard makes for the flakiest crust, others use only vegetable oil, and still others only use the kind that comes pre-made in a neat roll from the supermarket shelf (a viable option, if you're in a hurry). I prefer homemade piecrust to the store-bought variety, mostly because I'm not comfortable with the ingredients used in most prepackaged piecrusts. For the same reason, I like to stick to butter (rather than using lard or shortening)—I have no illusions about piecrust being healthy, but I'm convinced butter is a bit kinder to the body than hydrogenated fats or lard. Most any standard piecrust will work fine in your mini pie maker, but here I've included four of my preferred recipes (starting on page 1).

1. Pulse dry ingredients to mix.

2. Using chilled butter helps to keep the dough from sticking to your work surface and the rolling pin.

Using a food processor makes homemade piecrusts ridiculously easy. Here are the steps:

1. Place the flour and any other dry ingredients in the bowl of a food processor fitted with a steel blade. Pulse to mix.

2. Use chilled butter—straight out of the freezer is ideal—and cut it into small pieces. Add to the flour mixture.

3. Add very cold water one tablespoon at a time, pulsing after each addition. Eventually, dough will form into small crumbs. At this point, stop mixing. Over-mixing dough will make it tough.

4. Use hands to form dough into a ball. Flatten slightly into a disk. If not using immediately, seal in plastic wrap and store in the refrigerator. Remove from refrigerator a couple minutes before rolling out.

3. When dough begins to stick together, stop mixing.

4. Gather the dough into a ball and flatten it slightly on a lightly floured work surface.

5. Don't worry if your dough isn't a perfect circle—once it's cut into mini pie crusts, no one will know the difference.

5. Cover a large board or work surface with a thin layer of flour. Roll the dough from the center outward, rotating the angle of the rolling pin to make a relatively even circle of dough. If the rolling pin sticks to the dough, dust the dough lightly with flour. Stop rolling when the dough is between ⅛" and ¼" thick.

6. Cut dough into circles to fit pie maker or muffin tins. Gather dough scraps to form a ball and roll out again.

The recipes here each make enough for four single-crust mini pies. If you will be making four double-crust pies, you'll need to make two batches.

> To make crusts extra golden: just before baking, brush dough with a little cream or an egg whisked with a teaspoon of water.

Once you've cut as many pastry rounds as possible, gather the scraps and roll out the dough again.

6. Many mini pie maker appliances come with a cutter so you can get the crusts just the right size.

Pre-baking Piecrusts

To make a shell for a tart or a pie with a filling that doesn't need to be baked, you'll need to pre-bake, or "blind bake," your bottom crusts.

Roll out the dough and cut out bottom crust rounds.

Line mini pie maker or muffin tins with bottom piecrusts for 4 pies and press down to form indents.

Cover with dried beans or pie weights to hold the crust in place. Bake in a mini pie maker or in an oven preheated to 400 degrees for 4 to 6 minutes, or until crusts are golden.

Use a plastic spatula or other utensil to remove crusts from pie maker or muffin tins. Place on a large plate or baking tray.

Spread dried beans or pie weights evenly over the bottom to keep the crust from puffing up while baking.

When the crust is golden around the edges, it's ready to be removed.

Lattice Top Crusts

Lattice top crusts reveal a bit of the pie's filling, creating a pretty and colorful little pie. To create a simple lattice top, cut the dough into rounds as usual. Then slice the round into five strips. Place three of the strips in one direction and two in the opposite direction. You can weave the strips, or simply leave them crisscrossed.

{ PIECRUST RECIPES }

All Butter Piecrust

Ingredients

1 ¼ cups all-purpose flour   ½ teaspoon salt
½ cup unsalted butter, cold   3 to 4 tablespoons ice water

Directions

Combine flour and salt in a food processor fitted with a steel blade and pulse to mix. Cut butter into ½ inch pieces, add to flour mixture, and pulse until mixture forms a coarse meal. Add ice water a little at a time, pulsing until dough begins to hold together.

Chocolate Piecrust

Ingredients

1 ¼ cups all-purpose flour

3 tablespoons unsweetened cocoa
   powder

2 tablespoons sugar

½ cup unsalted butter, cold

½ teaspoon salt

3 to 5 tablespoons ice water

Directions

Combine flour, salt, cocoa powder, and sugar in a food processor fitted with a steel blade and pulse to mix. Cut butter into ½ inch pieces, add to flour mixture, and pulse until mixture forms a coarse meal. Add ice water a little at a time, pulsing until dough begins to hold together.

Whole Wheat Piecrust

Ingredients

1 ½ cups whole wheat pastry flour

2 teaspoons sugar

½ teaspoon salt

½ cup butter, cold

4 to 5 tablespoons cold milk

Directions

Combine flour, sugar, and salt in a food processor fitted with a steel blade and pulse to mix. Cut butter into ½ inch pieces, add to flour mixture, and pulse until mixture forms a coarse meal. Add cold milk a little at a time, pulsing until dough begins to hold together.

Gluten-Free Piecrust

MAKES 4 SINGLE-CRUST MINI PIES.

Ingredients

1 cup white rice flour

¼ cup potato starch (not potato flour)

¼ cup tapioca starch

1 teaspoon xanthan gum

1 teaspoon salt

2 tablespoons sugar

½ cup butter, cold

2 to 4 tablespoons ice water

Directions

Combine all dry ingredients in a food processor fitted with a steel blade and pulse to mix. Cut butter into ½ inch pieces, add to flour mixture, and pulse until mixture forms a coarse meal. Add ice water a little at a time, pulsing until dough begins to hold together.

Remove the dough from the food processor and form into a ball. Flatten it slightly, wrap in plastic wrap, and refrigerate for at least one hour. Remove from refrigerator a few minutes before ready to use. Roll the dough between two pieces of waxed paper sprinkled with gluten-free flour.

{ SAVORY PIES }

Spinach Pizza Pies

Ingredients

Pastry for 4 bottom crusts

Sauce

1 6-ounce can tomato paste

¼ teaspoon oregano

¼ teaspoon basil

⅛ teaspoon salt

3 tablespoon water

Toppings

8 leaves of baby spinach

½ cup shredded mozzarella

Directions

Line mini pie maker or muffin tins with bottom piecrusts for 4 pies.

Combine all ingredients for the sauce and spread a thin layer over each of the 4 crusts.

Place two spinach leaves on each pie and cover with a thick layer of shredded cheese.

Bake for 6 to 10 minutes in your mini pie maker or 10 to 15 minutes in an oven preheated to 400 degrees. Remove when crust is golden and cheese is bubbly.

Slow Cooker Steak and Guinness Pies

Ingredients

Pastry for 4 top and bottom crusts

½ pound beef chuck, cut into small cubes

¼ cup flour

1 teaspoon salt

½ teaspoon pepper

1 small carrot, diced

½ onion, peeled and diced

1 small potato, diced

2 cloves garlic, peeled and finely diced

½ teaspoon dried thyme

½ teaspoon fresh rosemary, finely chopped

1 12-ounce bottle Guinness

½ teaspoon mustard powder

½ cup beef or vegetable broth

Directions

Combine flour, salt, and pepper in a bowl and toss beef cubes to coat.

Place beef and all remaining ingredients in a slow cooker. Cover and cook on low for 5-6 hours.

When beef filling is done, line mini pie maker or muffin tins with bottom piecrusts for 4 pies. Fill each crust about ⅔ full with beef filling. If filling is very juicy, use a slotted spoon to drain off some of the liquid before putting it in the crust.

Cover with top crusts and bake in mini pie maker for 10 to 12 minutes or in an oven preheated to 400 degrees for 15 to 17 minutes or until crust is golden.

Basil Tomato Tarts

Ingredients

Pastry for 4 bottom crusts

¼ cup shredded Gruyere, fresh mozzarella, or ricotta cheese

1 medium tomato, sliced

8 leaves of basil

2 tablespoons balsamic vinegar

Sea salt and freshly ground pepper to taste

Directions

Line mini pie maker or muffin tins with bottom piecrusts for 4 pies.

Spread cheese over crusts. Place one or two slices of tomato in the bottom of each pie, then layer a couple leaves of basil on top.

Drizzle the balsamic vinegar over each tart. Bake in a mini pie maker for 8 to 10 minutes or in an oven preheated to 400 degrees for 12 to 15 minutes or until the crusts are golden.

Add salt and pepper to taste.

Shepherd's Pies

Ingredients

Pastry for 4 bottom crusts
½ pound ground beef
⅓ onion, finely chopped
1 cup frozen carrots and peas
2 medium potatoes

3 tablespoons butter
½ teaspoon Worcestershire sauce
⅛ teaspoon black pepper
⅛ teaspoon salt
2 tablespoons cream

Directions

Peel and quarter potatoes and boil in salted water until tender (about 15 minutes).

Line mini pie maker or muffin tins with bottom piecrusts for 4 pies.

Heat 1 tablespoon butter in a saucepan and sauté onions until translucent. Add beef and continue to cook, stirring frequently, until fully browned. Add vegetables, Worcestershire sauce, and pepper.

Mash potatoes with 2 tablespoons butter, cream, and salt

Fill each piecrust about ⅔ full and dollop about 2 tablespoons of mashed potato on top of each.

Bake for 8 to 10 minutes in a mini pie maker or 12 to 15 minutes in an oven preheated to 400 degrees. When potato is golden, pies are ready.

Chicken Pot Pies

Ingredients

Pastry for 4 top and bottom crusts

2 cups cooked chicken, cut in small
pieces

2 tablespoons butter

¼ onion, finely diced

1 cup frozen mixed vegetables

½ cup milk or cream

2 tablespoons cornstarch

⅛ teaspoon rosemary

½ teaspoon celery seed

¼ teaspoon salt

⅛ teaspoon black pepper

Directions

Line mini pie maker or muffin tins with bottom piecrusts for 4 pies.

Heat butter in a saucepan and sauté onions until translucent. Whisk together milk or cream and cornstarch and pour into saucepan. Add seasonings.

When mixture is bubbling and beginning to thicken, add vegetables and cooked chicken. Simmer until vegetables are fully thawed and sauce is thick.

Divide filling between the 4 crusts. Cover with top crusts and bake in a mini pie maker for 10 to 12 minutes or in an oven preheated to 400 degrees for 15 to 17 minutes or until the crusts are golden.

Eggplant Parmesan Tarts

Ingredients

Pastry for 4 bottom crusts

For the Sauce:

1 tablespoon olive oil	1 teaspoon dried oregano
1 14.5-ounce can crushed tomatoes	1 teaspoon dried basil
1 clove garlic, peeled and minced	½ teaspoon salt
¼ onion, peeled and diced	½ teaspoon sugar

For the Eggplant:

1 small eggplant	⅛ teaspoon black pepper
1 cup breadcrumbs	2 eggs, beaten
½ teaspoon parsley	1 tablespoon water
1 teaspoon oregano	Oil for frying
¼ teaspoon salt	⅔ cup shredded mozzarella

To make the sauce, heat the olive oil in a saucepan and add the garlic and onions, simmering until the onions become translucent. Add the remaining sauce ingredients and simmer for about twenty minutes.

Slice eggplant into ¼" thick pieces. Combine flour and herbs in one bowl and place the breadcrumbs in a separate bowl with a wide bottom. Whisk together eggs and water in a third bowl.

Dredge each piece of eggplant in the flour mixture, then dip in the egg, and then coat with breadcrumbs.

Heat ½ inch of oil in a pan until bubbling. Drop eggplant slices in and fry, turning once, for about 3 minutes or until golden. Use tongs to transfer to a paper towel-lined plate.

Line mini pie maker or muffin tins with bottom piecrusts for 4 pies. Spread a layer of sauce, then one or two pieces of eggplant, then more sauce, and finally cover with cheese.

Bake in a mini pie maker or in an oven preheated to 400 degrees 10 to 17 minutes or until cheese is golden and bubbly.

Spinach Mushroom Quiches

Ingredients

Pastry for 4 bottom crusts

1 tablespoon butter

¼ onion, finely diced

4 eggs, lightly beaten

½ cup milk or cream

⅔ cup spinach, chopped (fresh or thawed)

¼ cup sliced mushrooms

¼ teaspoon salt

⅛ teaspoon black pepper

⅛ teaspoon nutmeg

½ cup shredded cheese (Swiss, Cheddar, or Monterey Jack)

Directions

Line mini pie maker or muffin tins with bottom piecrusts for 4 pies.

Heat butter in a saucepan and sauté onions until translucent. Add mushrooms and spinach and sauté until soft.

In a mixing bowl, combine eggs and milk or cream. Add seasonings and vegetables.

Ladle mixture into bottom crusts, filling each about ⅔ to ¾ full. Sprinkle cheese over the top.

Bake about 10 minutes in a mini pie maker or about 20 minutes in a 350 degree oven, or until filling is set. To tell if the eggs are cooked through, stick a toothpick in the center of one quiche and see if it comes out mostly dry.

Cracked Egg Pies

Ingredients

Pastry for 4 bottom crusts

4 eggs

Salt and pepper to taste

6 leaves baby spinach

4 tomato slices (optional)

4 slices cooked ham (optional)

Shredded cheese (optional)

Directions

Line mini pie maker or muffin tins with bottom piecrusts for 4 pies.

If desired, place spinach leaves, a tomato slice, or slice of ham in the bottom of each crust.

Crack an egg into a measuring cup with a spout and then pour it into the crust. Repeat with the other three pies. Sprinkle with cheese, salt, and pepper as desired.

Bake for 8 to 10 minutes in a mini pie maker or about 12 minutes in a 350 degree oven, or until eggs are set and crust is golden.

Spicy Chicken and Cheese Empanadas

Ingredients

Pastry for 4 bottom crusts

1 cup cooked chicken, cut in small pieces

½ cup shredded Colby, Monterey Jack, or Swiss cheese (or combination)

2 tablespoons cream cheese

1 inch jalapeno, finely diced

1 small roasted red pepper, drained and finely diced

½ teaspoon cumin

¼ teaspoon salt

⅛ teaspoon black pepper

Directions

Line mini pie maker or muffin tins with bottom piecrusts for 4 pies.

Combine chicken and remaining ingredients. Fill each pie ⅔ full and cover with top piecrusts.

Bake in a mini pie maker for 8 to 10 minutes or in an oven preheated to 400 degrees for 12 to 15 minutes or until the crusts are golden.

Black Bean and Plantain Empanadas

Ingredients

Pastry for 4 bottom crusts

1 tablespoon oil

1 small ripe plantain, coarsely
   chopped

3 tablespoons onion, diced

1 cup black beans, drained and
   rinsed

2 tablespoons fresh cilantro, minced

½ teaspoon cumin

¼ teaspoon lime juice

¼ teaspoon salt

⅛ teaspoon black pepper

Directions

Line mini pie maker or muffin tins with bottom piecrusts for 4 pies.

Heat olive oil in a saucepan. Saute onion and plantain until onions are translucent and plantains are soft (about 5 minutes)

Remove from heat and combine with all remaining ingredients.

Fill each pie ⅔ full and cover with top piecrusts.

Bake in a mini pie maker for 8 to 10 minutes or in an oven preheated to 400 degrees for 12 to 15 minutes or until the crusts are golden.

Cornish Pasties

Ingredients

Pastry for 4 top and bottom crusts

1 cup cubed cooked steak, roast beef, or other beef cut

1 medium potato, diced

1 tablespoon butter

¼ cup diced onions

¼ cup diced carrots

¼ cup diced Swede or rutabaga

¼ cup cream

¼ teaspoon salt

⅛ teaspoon pepper

Directions

Boil the potatoes, Swede or rutabaga, and carrots until tender (about 15 minutes). Drain.

Meanwhile, heat the butter in a saucepan and sauté the onions until translucent. Add the cream and the beef and cook just until warmed through.

Combine the meat and onions with the other vegetables and fill each pie ⅔ full. Cover with top piecrusts and bake in a mini pie maker for 10 to 12 minutes or in an oven preheated to 400 degrees for 15 to 17 minutes or until the crusts are golden.

FRUIT AND BERRY PIES

Apple Pies

Ingredients

Pastry for 4 top and bottom crusts

2 tablespoons butter

3 medium apples, cored, peeled, and sliced

½ teaspoon cinnamon

⅛ teaspoon nutmeg

½ cup brown sugar

1 tablespoon cornstarch

⅛ teaspoon salt

Directions

In a medium bowl, combine brown sugar, cinnamon, nutmeg, cornstarch, and salt.

Heat butter in a large skillet, add sliced apples, and cook for about 3 minutes. Add brown sugar mixture and continue to cook for 2 to 3 minutes, or until apples are soft.

Line mini pie maker or muffin tins with bottom piecrusts for 4 pies. Divide apples between the four pies. Cover with top crusts and bake in a mini pie maker for 10 to 12 minutes or in an oven preheated to 400 degrees for 15 to 17 minutes or until the crusts are golden.

Ginger Peach Pies

Ingredients

Pastry for 4 top and bottom crusts

1 15.25-ounce can peaches in fruit juice (not syrup)

3 tablespoons brown sugar

2 tablespoons cornstarch

½ teaspoon ground ginger

½ teaspoon lemon juice

1 tablespoon butter

2 tablespoons crystallized ginger, finely chopped (optional)

Directions

In a medium bowl, combine brown sugar, cornstarch, and ground ginger.

Drain peaches, slice, and add to brown sugar mixture. Add lemon juice and crystallized ginger, if using. Toss to coat peaches.

Line mini pie maker or muffin tins with bottom piecrusts for 4 pies. Divide peaches between the four pies. Dot each pie with pats of butter.

Cover with top crusts and bake in a mini pie maker for 10 to 12 minutes or in an oven preheated to 400 degrees for 15 to 17 minutes or until the crusts are golden.

Caramelized Pear Pies

Ingredients

Pastry for 4 top and bottom crusts

1 15.25 oz can pears in fruit juice (not syrup)

3 tablespoons brown sugar

2 tablespoons cornstarch

1 teaspoon cinnamon

⅛ teaspoon salt

½ teaspoon lemon zest (optional)

1 tablespoon butter

Directions

In a medium bowl, combine brown sugar, cornstarch, cinnamon, salt, and lemon zest (if using).

Drain pears, slice, and add to brown sugar mixture. Toss to coat pears.

Line mini pie maker or muffin tins with bottom piecrusts for 4 pies. Divide pears between the four pies. Dot each pie with pats of butter.

Cover with top crusts and bake in a mini pie maker for 10 to 12 minutes or in an oven preheated to 400 degrees for 15 to 17 minutes or until the crusts are golden.

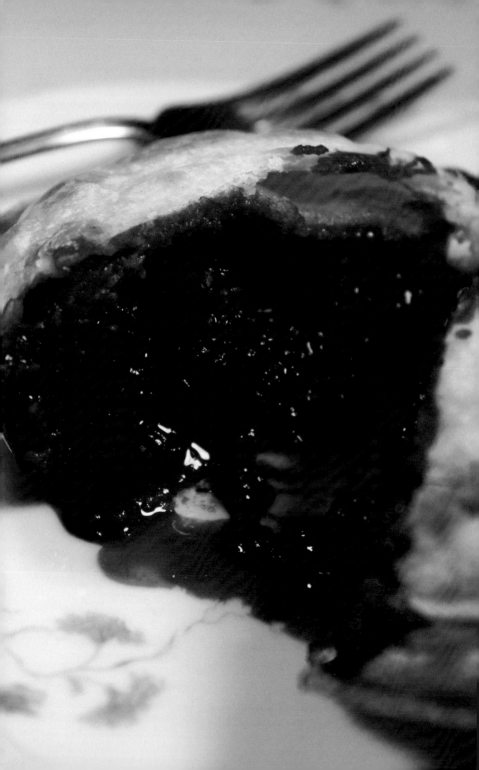

Blackberry Malbec Pies

Ingredients

Pastry for 4 top and bottom crusts

2 cups blackberries (fresh or fully thawed)

1 tablespoon cornstarch

1 tablespoon flour

3 tablespoons granulated sugar

2 tablespoons malbec or other red wine

1 teaspoon vanilla extract

Directions

Mix together cornstarch, flour, and sugar. Add the blackberries, malbec, and vanilla and mix together to coat the berries.

Line mini pie maker or muffin tins with bottom piecrusts for 4 pies. Use a slotted spoon to divide the filling between the four pie bases, allowing excess liquid to strain off for a moment before placing in the pies.

Cover with top crusts and bake in a mini pie maker for 10 to 12 minutes or in an oven preheated to 400 degrees for 15 to 17 minutes or until the crusts are golden.

Blueberry Almond Pies

Ingredients

Pastry for 4 top and bottom crusts

2 cups blueberries (fresh or fully thawed)

1 tablespoon cornstarch

1 tablespoon flour

3 tablespoons granulated sugar

½ teaspoon cinnamon

¼ cup sliced almonds

Directions

Mix together the cornstarch, flour, sugar, and cinnamon. Add the blueberries and almonds and mix to coat the berries.

Line mini pie maker or muffin tins with bottom piecrusts for 4 pies. Use a slotted spoon to divide the filling between the 4 pie bases, allowing excess liquid to strain off for a moment before placing in the pies.

Cover with top crusts and bake in a mini pie maker for 10 to 12 minutes or in an oven preheated to 400 degrees for 15 to 17 minutes or until the crusts are golden.

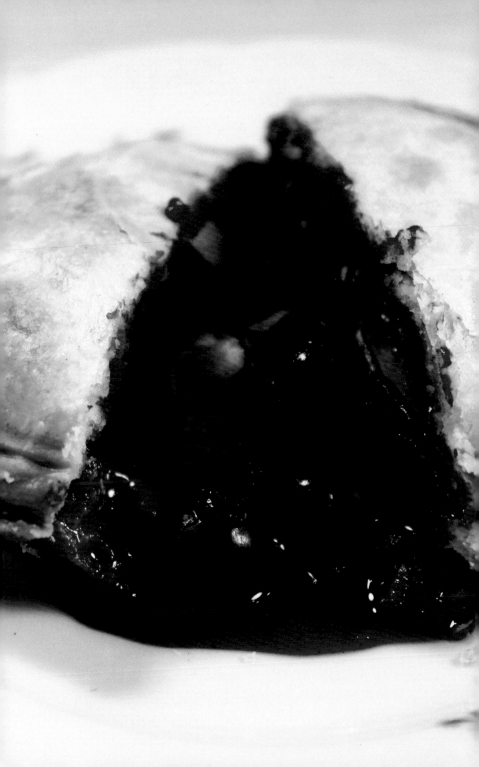

Holiday Raisin Pies

Ingredients

Pastry for 4 top and bottom crusts

2 cups raisins

1 ½ cups water

2-3 tablespoons brandy or rum

½ cup brown sugar

2 tablespoons cornstarch

½ teaspoon cinnamon

¼ teaspoon salt

1 teaspoon grated orange peel

1 tablespoon butter

Directions

Line mini pie maker or muffin tins with bottom piecrusts for 4 pies.

In a small saucepan, heat raisins and water to boiling. Allow to boil for about 5 minutes. Meanwhile, combine brown sugar, cornstarch, cinnamon, and salt.

Add brown sugar mixture and brandy or rum to raisins and continue to simmer until the sugar gets syrupy.

Remove from heat, add butter cut into small pieces and orange peel, stir, and divide filling between piecrusts.

Cut top pastry rounds into strips and form a lattice top over each pie. Bake in a mini pie maker for 8 to 10 minutes or in an oven preheated to 400 degrees for 12 to 15 minutes or until the crusts are golden.

Plum Tarts with Citrus Cream

Ingredients

Pastry for 4 bottom crusts

4 medium plums, pitted and sliced

½ cup granulated sugar

1 teaspoon lemon juice

½ teaspoon cinnamon

1 cup heavy or whipping cream

2 tablespoons honey

2 tablespoons grated lemon or
    orange peel

Directions

Line mini pie maker or muffin tins with bottom piecrusts for 4 pies.

In a skillet, sauté sliced plums with the sugar, cinnamon, and lemon juice for 3 to 5 minutes, or until the plums are warm and soft.

Divide filling evenly between crusts and bake in a mini pie maker for 8 to 10 minutes or in an oven preheated to 400 degrees for 12 to 15 minutes, or until the crusts are golden. Remove tarts from pie maker or pans and place on serving plates.

Beat the cream until it begins to stiffen. Add honey in a thin stream, continuing to beat until soft peaks form when you lift the beaters. Fold in grated citrus peel.

Place a big dollop of cream over each tart just before serving.

Easy Pumpkin Pies

Ingredients

Pastry for 4 bottom crusts

1 15-ounce can pumpkin puree

2 tablespoons heavy cream or condensed milk

⅔ cup brown sugar

1 teaspoon pumpkin pie spice (or
equal parts cinnamon, ginger,
and nutmeg)

¼ teaspoon salt

1 teaspoon vanilla

Whipped cream, for serving

Directions

Line mini pie maker or muffin tins with bottom piecrusts for 4 pies.

Mix together the pumpkin, cream, brown sugar, pumpkin pie spice, salt, and vanilla.

Divide filling evenly between crusts and bake in a mini pie maker for 8 to 10 minutes or in an oven preheated to 400 degrees for 12 to 15 minutes or until the crusts are golden.

Strawberry Rhubarb Pies

Ingredients

Pastry for 4 top and bottom crusts

2 cups chopped rhubarb

1 cup strawberries, hulled and sliced

1 cup granulated sugar

1 tablespoon butter

Directions

Line mini pie maker or muffin tins with bottom piecrusts for 4 pies.

In a saucepan, heat rhubarb and sugar and simmer for about 10 minutes, or until the rhubarb starts to become soft. Add strawberries and simmer for another 3 to 4 minutes. Add butter and mix until melted and combined. Remove from heat.

Divide filling between crusts. Slice top pastry rounds into strips to create a lattice top over each pie.

Bake in a mini pie maker for 8 to 10 minutes or in an oven preheated to 400 degrees for 12 to 15 minutes, or until the crusts are golden.

Cherry Pies

Ingredients

Pastry for 4 top and bottom crusts

2 cups pitted tart cherries (fresh or frozen)

2 tablespoons cornstarch

½ cup granulated sugar

⅛ teaspoon salt

1 teaspoon lemon juice

¼ teaspoon almond or vanilla extract

Directions

Line mini pie maker or muffin tins with bottom piecrusts for 4 pies.

In a medium saucepan, cook the cherries with the cornstarch, sugar, salt, lemon juice, and almond or vanilla extract for about five minutes.

Divide filling between crusts. Slice top pastry rounds into strips to create a lattice top over each pie.

Bake in a mini pie maker for 8 to 10 minutes or in an oven preheated to 400 degrees for 12 to 15 minutes, or until the crusts are golden.

Sweet Potato Pies

Ingredients

Pastry for 4 bottom crusts

2 cups cooked, mashed sweet potato

2 tablespoons heavy cream or condensed milk

⅔ cup brown sugar

½ teaspoon cinnamon

¼ teaspoon nutmeg

¼ teaspoon salt

1 teaspoon vanilla

Whipped cream, for serving

Directions

Line mini pie maker or muffin tins with bottom piecrusts for 4 pies.

Mix together the sweet potato, cream, brown sugar, cinnamon, nutmeg, salt, and vanilla.

Divide filling evenly between crusts and bake in a mini pie maker for 8 to 10 minutes or in an oven preheated to 400 degrees for 12 to 15 minutes, or until the crusts are golden. Serve with whipped cream.

Banana Dulce de Leche Pies

Ingredients

Pastry for 4 bottom crusts

1 8-ounce package cream cheese, room temperature

1 cup powdered sugar

½ cup whipping cream

1 cup dulce de leche

1 medium banana

Directions

Line mini pie maker or muffin tins with bottom piecrusts for 4 pies. Press down to form indents and cover with dried beans or pie weights to hold the crust in place. Bake in a mini pie maker for 4 to 6 minutes or in an oven preheated to 400 degrees for 8 to 12 minutes, or until crusts are golden.

Remove crusts from pie maker or muffin tins and place on a large plate or baking tray.

In a mixing bowl, beat the cream cheese until fluffy. Add the powdered sugar gradually, and then the whipping cream, continuing to beat until light and fluffy.

Spread ¼ cup dulce de leche in the bottom of each crust. Then divide filling between the pies. Chill for a couple hours. Just before serving, slice banana and arrange over the top of each pie.

Mixed Berry Pies

Ingredients

Pastry for 4 top and bottom crusts

2 cups blueberries, raspberries, blackberries, and/or strawberries

2 tablespoons cornstarch

¼ cup granulated sugar

½ teaspoon cinnamon

Directions

Mix together the cornstarch, sugar, and cinnamon. Add the berries and mix to coat.

Line mini pie maker or muffin tins with bottom piecrusts for 4 pies. Use a slotted spoon to divide the filling between the four pie bases, allowing excess liquid to strain off for a moment before placing in the pies.

Cover with top crusts and bake in a mini pie maker for 8 to 10 minutes or in an oven preheated to 400 degrees for 12 to 15 minutes, or until the crusts are golden.

Blueberry Crisp

Ingredients

Pastry for 4 bottom crusts   2 cups blueberries, fresh or thawed

Topping:
¾ cup oats   ½ teaspoon cinnamon

¾ cup all-purpose flour   ½ cup butter, melted

¾ cup brown sugar

Directions

Line mini pie maker or muffin tins with bottom piecrusts for 4 pies. Divide the blueberries between crusts.

In a medium-sized mixing bowl, combine oats, flour, brown sugar, and cinnamon. Pour melted butter over the top and stir.

Cover pies with topping and bake in a mini pie maker for 8 to 10 minutes or in an oven preheated to 400 degrees for 12 to 15 minutes, or until the crusts are golden.

Peach-Raspberry Pies

Ingredients

Pastry for 4 top and bottom crusts

2 tablespoons cornstarch

½ cup granulated sugar

¼ teaspoon cinnamon

1 cup raspberries (fresh or fully thawed)

1 cup peeled and sliced peaches

1 teaspoon lemon juice

Directions

Mix together the cornstarch, sugar, and cinnamon. Add the raspberries, peaches, and lemon juice. Mix to coat the fruit.

Line mini pie maker or muffin tins with bottom piecrusts for 4 pies. Use a slotted spoon to divide the filling between the four pie bases, allowing excess liquid to strain off for a moment before placing in the pies.

Cover with top crusts and bake in a mini pie maker for 8 to 10 minutes or in an oven preheated to 400 degrees for 12 to 15 minutes, or until the crusts are golden.

Rhubarb Crisp

Ingredients

Pastry for 4 bottom crusts

3 cups chopped rhubarb

1 cup granulated sugar

1 tablespoon butter

Topping:

¾ cup oats

¾ cup all-purpose flour

¾ cup brown sugar

½ teaspoon cinnamon

½ cup butter, melted

Directions

Line mini pie maker or muffin tins with bottom piecrusts for 4 pies.

In a saucepan, heat rhubarb and sugar and simmer for about 10 minutes, or until the rhubarb starts to become soft. Add butter and mix until melted and combined. Remove from heat.

Divide filling between crusts.

In a medium-sized mixing bowl, combine oats, flour, brown sugar, and cinnamon. Pour melted butter over the top and stir.

Cover pies with topping and bake in a mini pie maker for 8 to 10 minutes or in an oven preheated to 400 degrees for 12 to 15 minutes, or until the crusts are golden.

Blackberry Pies with Honey Lavender Cream

Ingredients

Pastry for 4 top and bottom crusts

2 cups blackberries (fresh or fully thawed)

2 tablespoons cornstarch

¼ cup granulated sugar

1 teaspoon vanilla extract

1 cup heavy or whipping cream

2 tablespoons honey

1 teaspoon lavender petals

Directions

Mix together the cornstarch, flour, and sugar. Add the blackberries, malbec, and vanilla and mix together to coat the berries.

Line mini pie maker or muffin tins with bottom piecrusts for 4 pies. Use a slotted spoon to divide the filling between the four pie bases, allowing excess liquid to strain off for a moment before placing in the pies.

Cover with top crusts and bake in a mini pie maker for 8 to 10 minutes or in an oven preheated to 400 degrees for 12 to 15 minutes, or until the crusts are golden.

To make the whipped cream, put cream in a bowl and beat until it begins to thicken. Drizzle honey in and continue to beat until soft peaks form. Fold in lavender petals just before serving.

Triple Berry Crisp

Ingredients

Pastry for 4 bottom crusts

2 cups blueberries, raspberries, and blackberries, fresh or thawed

Topping:

¾ cup oats

¾ cup all-purpose flour

¾ cup brown sugar

½ teaspoon cinnamon

½ cup butter, melted

Directions

Line mini pie maker or muffin tins with bottom piecrusts for 4 pies. Divide the berries between crusts.

In a medium-sized mixing bowl, combine oats, flour, brown sugar, and cinnamon. Pour melted butter over the top and stir.

Cover pies with topping and bake in a mini pie maker for 8 to 10 minutes or in an oven preheated to 400 degrees for 12 to 15 minutes, or until the crusts are golden.

American Flag Pies

Ingredients

Pastry for 4 top and bottom crusts

2 tablespoons cornstarch

½ cup granulated sugar

¼ teaspoon cinnamon

1 ½ cups strawberries, sliced (fresh or fully thawed)

1 cup blueberries

1 teaspoon lemon juice

Directions

Place the strawberries and blueberries in separate bowls. Mix together the cornstarch, sugar, and cinnamon, and put ⅔ of the mixture in with the strawberries and ⅓ with the blueberries. Mix each to coat the fruit.

Line mini pie maker or muffin tins with bottom piecrusts for 4 pies. Imagine each pie divided into quarters and place the strawberries in the bottom and top right quadrants. Place the blueberries in the top left quadrant.

Cut the top pastry rounds into strips and stars. Place the strips horizontally over the strawberry sections and the stars over the blueberries. Bake in a mini pie maker for 8 to 10 minutes or in an oven preheated to 400 degrees for 12 to 15 minutes, or until the crusts are golden.

Old-Fashioned Quince Pies

Ingredients

Pastry for 4 top and bottom crusts

3 medium quinces, cored, peeled, and sliced

⅓ cup honey

1 cup water

2 tablespoons cornstarch

⅓ cup granulated sugar

½ teaspoon cinnamon

⅛ teaspoon salt

1 tablespoon butter

Directions

In a medium saucepan, combine the quince slices, honey, and water. Bring to a slow boil and cook for about 5 minutes, or until quinces soften. Strain the fruit, reserving the liquid.

In a mixing bowl, combine the cornstarch, sugar, cinnamon, salt, and butter. Combine with the reserved liquid in a saucepan and bring do a boil, stirring constantly. Simmer for a couple minutes until the sauce thickens. Pour over fruit and mix.

Line mini pie maker or muffin tins with bottom piecrusts for 4 pies. Divide fruit between pies, cover with top crusts, and bake in a mini pie maker for 8 to 10 minutes or in an oven preheated to 400 degrees for 12 to 15 minutes, or until the crusts are golden.

Easy Yogurt Berry Tarts

Ingredients

Pastry for 4 bottom crusts   1 cup fresh berries
2 cups yogurt (any flavor or variety)

Directions

Line mini pie maker or muffin tins with bottom piecrusts for 4 pies. Press down to form indents, and cover with dried beans or pie weights to hold the crust in place. Bake in a mini pie maker for 4 to 6 minutes or in an oven preheated to 400 degrees for 8 to 12 minutes, or until crusts are golden.

Remove crusts from pie maker or muffin tins and place on a large plate or baking tray.

Just before serving, divide yogurt between crusts and cover with fresh berries.

Blueberry Peach Crisp

Ingredients

Pastry for 4 bottom crusts

Filling:

1 cup blueberries   ½ cup sugar

1 cup sliced peaches   2 tablespoons cornstarch

Topping:

¾ cup oats   ½ teaspoon cinnamon

¾ cup all-purpose flour   ½ cup butter, melted

¾ cup brown sugar

Directions

Mix together the cornstarch and sugar. Add the blueberries and peaches. Mix to coat the fruit.

Line mini pie maker or muffin tins with bottom piecrusts for 4 pies. Divide the filling between the pies.

In a medium-sized mixing bowl, combine oats, flour, brown sugar, and cinnamon. Pour melted butter over the top and stir.

Cover pies with topping and bake in a mini pie maker for 8 to 10 minutes or in an oven preheated to 400 degrees for 12 to 15 minutes, or until the crusts are golden.

Apple Walnut Crisp

Ingredients

Pastry for 4 bottom crusts

Filling:
2 tablespoons butter

1 ½ cups peeled, cored, and sliced apples

½ cup brown sugar

½ cup halved or crushed walnuts

Topping:
¾ cup oats

¾ cup all-purpose flour

¾ cup brown sugar

½ teaspoon cinnamon

½ cup butter, melted

Directions

Heat butter in a large skillet, add sliced apples, and cook for about 3 minutes. Add brown sugar mixture and continue to cook for 2 to 3 minutes, or until apples are soft. Remove from heat and mix in walnuts.

Line mini pie maker or muffin tins with bottom piecrusts for 4 pies. Divide the filling between the pies.

In a medium-sized mixing bowl, combine oats, flour, brown sugar, and cinnamon. Pour melted butter over the top and stir.

Cover pies with topping and bake in a mini pie maker for 8 to 10 minutes or in an oven preheated to 400 degrees for 12 to 15 minutes, or until the crusts are golden.

Pineapple Coconut Tarts

Ingredients

Pastry for 4 bottom crusts

1 14-ounce can condensed milk

1 cup granulated sugar

2 tablespoons cornstarch

⅛ teaspoon salt

½ cup coconut flakes

½ cup crushed pineapple, drained

Whipped cream, for serving

Directions

Line mini pie maker or muffin tins with bottom piecrusts for 4 pies. Press down to form indents, and cover with dried beans or pie weights to hold the crust in place. Bake in a mini pie maker for 4 to 6 minutes or in an oven preheated to 400 degrees for 8 to 12 minutes, or until crusts are golden.

Remove crusts from pie maker or muffin tins and place on a large plate or baking tray.

Combine condensed milk, sugar, cornstarch, and salt in a saucepan and stir over low heat until mixture begins to thicken (about 5 to 6 minutes). Remove from heat and fold in coconut flakes and crushed pineapple. Divide filling between crusts and chill for about 2 hours before serving. Dollop whipped cream over each pie just before serving.

Strawberry "Shortcakes"

Ingredients

Pastry for 4 bottom crusts

Filling:

2 cups sliced strawberries, fresh or thawed

1 tablespoon cornstarch

½ cup sugar

Topping:

¾ cup all-purpose flour

1 tablespoon sugar

1 teaspoon baking powder

¼ teaspoon salt

2 tablespoons butter

⅓ cup heavy cream

Whipped cream, for serving

Directions

Mix together cornstarch and sugar, add sliced strawberries, and toss to coat.

To make the topping, mix together the flour, sugar, baking powder, and salt. Cut the butter into small pieces and use your fingers to work it into the flour. Mixture will still be lumpy. Add the cream and mix to form a soft dough.

Line mini pie maker or muffin tins with bottom piecrusts for 4 pies. Divide the filling between the pies.

Spoon the topping over each pie. Bake in a mini pie maker for 8 to 10 minutes or in an oven preheated to 400 degrees for 12 to 15 minutes, or until the crusts are golden. Serve with whipped cream.

Pineapple Pies

Ingredients

Pastry for 4 top and bottom crusts

1 20-ounce can crushed pineapple
   with juice

3 tablespoons cornstarch

1 tablespoon lemon juice

½ cup brown sugar

Directions

In a medium saucepan, heat all ingredients for several minutes, stirring constantly until thick.

Line mini pie maker or muffin tins with bottom piecrusts for 4 pies. Divide the filling between the four pie bases.

Cover with top crusts and bake in a mini pie maker for 8 to 10 minutes or in an oven preheated to 400 degrees for 12 to 15 minutes, or until the crusts are golden.

Apple Raisin Tarts

Ingredients

Pastry for 4 bottom crusts

2 tablespoons butter

1-½ cups apple slices

½ cup raisins

⅓ cup brown sugar

¼ teaspoon cinnamon

Directions

Line mini pie maker or muffin tins with bottom piecrusts for 4 pies. Press down to form indents, and cover with dried beans or pie weights to hold the crust in place. Bake in a mini pie maker for 4 to 6 minutes or in an oven preheated to 400 degrees for 8 to 12 minutes, or until crusts are golden.

Remove crusts from pie maker or muffin tins and place on a large plate or baking tray.

Heat butter in a large skillet. Saute apple slices and raisins with the brown sugar and cinnamon until apples are soft.

Spoon filling into the pie shells just before serving.

Easy Key Lime Pie

Ingredients

Pastry for 4 bottom crusts

3 egg yolks, lightly beaten

1 14-ounce can sweetened condensed milk

½ cup lime juice

Whipped cream, for serving

1 teaspoon finely grated lime zest

Directions

Line mini pie maker or muffin tins with bottom piecrusts for 4 pies.

Combine beaten egg yolks, sweetened condensed milk, and lime juice. Pour into pastry shells.

Bake in a mini pie maker for 10 to 12 minutes or in an oven preheated to 400 degrees for 14 to 17 minutes, or until the crusts are golden. Remove and chill for at least 2 hours.

Just before serving, cover pies with whipped cream and sprinkle with lime zest.

CHOCOLATE, CREAM, NUT, AND OTHER DELICIOUS PIES

Apple Cream Cheese Crumble

Ingredients

Pastry for 4 bottom crusts

Filling:

2 medium apples, cored, peeled, and sliced

2 tablespoons butter

4 ounces (½ package) cream cheese, room temperature

⅔ cup confectioner's sugar

¼ cup brown sugar

½ teaspoon cinnamon

1 teaspoon cornstarch

Topping:

¾ cup oats

¾ cup all-purpose flour

¾ cup brown sugar

½ teaspoon cinnamon

½ cup butter, melted

Directions

In a large mixing bowl, beat together cream cheese and confectioner's sugar.

In a separate bowl, combine brown sugar, cinnamon, and cornstarch.

Heat butter in a large skillet, add sliced apples, and cook for about three minutes. Add brown sugar mixture and continue to cook for 2 to 3 minutes, or until apples are soft.

Remove from heat and add apples to cream cheese mixture. Stir to coat apples.

Line mini pie maker or muffin tins with bottom piecrusts for 4 pies. Divide apples between the four pies.

In a medium mixing bowl, combine oats, flour, brown sugar, and cinnamon. Pour melted butter over the top and stir.

Divide topping between pies and bake in a mini pie maker for 8 to 10 minutes or in an oven preheated to 400 degrees for 12 to 15 minutes, or until the crusts are golden.

Chocolate Chip Cheesecakes

Ingredients

Pastry for 4 bottom crusts

1 8-ounce package cream cheese

1 14-ounce can sweetened condensed milk

1 tablespoon lemon juice

1 teaspoon vanilla

1 cup miniature chocolate chips

Directions

Line mini pie maker or muffin tins with bottom piecrusts for 4 pies. Press down to form indents, and cover with dried beans or pie weights to hold the crust in place. Bake in a mini pie maker or in an oven preheated to 400 degrees for 4 to 6 minutes, or until crusts are golden.

Remove crusts from pie maker or muffin tins and place on a large plate or baking tray.

In a mixing bowl, beat cream cheese until fluffy. Gradually add the condensed milk, lemon juice, and vanilla, blending until smooth. Add the chocolate chips and stir. Divide filling evenly between the four pies and refrigerate a couple hours or until set.

Mocha Souffles

Ingredients

Pastry for 4 bottom crusts

5 ounces bittersweet chocolate,
   chopped

1 tablespoon butter

½ cup sugar

2 tablespoons instant coffee
   granules

2 eggs

Whipped cream for serving

Directions

Line mini pie maker or muffin tins with bottom piecrusts for 4 pies.

Beat eggs until light and fluffy.

In a double boiler, melt chocolate and butter. Add sugar and coffee and mix. Remove from heat and fold in beaten eggs.

Use a ladle to divide filling between crusts. Bake in a mini pie maker for 8 to 10 minutes or in an oven preheated to 400 degrees for 12 to 15 minutes, or until the crusts are golden.

Serve with a dollop of whipped cream over each pie.

Maple Cream Pies

Ingredients

Pastry for 4 bottom crusts

1 14-ounce can condensed milk

¼ cup maple syrup

⅓ cup brown sugar

2 tablespoons cornstarch

⅛ teaspoon salt

Directions

Line mini pie maker or muffin tins with bottom piecrusts for 4 pies. Press down to form indents, and cover with dried beans or pie weights to hold the crust in place. Bake in a mini pie maker for 4 to 6 minutes or in an oven preheated to 400 degrees for 8 to 12 minutes, or until crusts are golden.

Remove crusts from pie maker or muffin tins and place on a large plate or baking tray.

Combine condensed milk, maple syrup, brown sugar, cornstarch, and salt in a saucepan and stir over low heat until mixture begins to thicken (about 5 to 6 minutes). Divide filling between crusts and chill for about 2 hours before serving.

Peanut Butter Chocolate Pies

Ingredients

Pastry for 4 bottom crusts

1 cup creamy peanut butter

1 8-ounce package cream cheese, room temperature

1 cup powdered sugar

1 teaspoon vanilla

⅔ cup chocolate chips (mini or regular)

Whipped cream, for topping

Directions

Line mini pie maker or muffin tins with bottom piecrusts for 4 pies. Press down to form indents, and cover with dried beans or pie weights to hold the crust in place. Bake in a mini pie maker for 4 to 6 minutes or in an oven preheated to 400 degrees for 8 to 12 minutes, or until crusts are golden.

In a mixing bowl, beat the peanut butter, cream cheese, and vanilla until fluffy. Add the powdered sugar gradually, continuing to beat. Fold in the chocolate chips.

Divide the filling between the pre-baked piecrusts and chill for a couple hours before serving. Serve with whipped cream.

Strawberries 'n' Cream Pies

Ingredients

Chocolate pastry for 4 bottom crusts (see page 4)

4 ounces (½ package) cream cheese

½ teaspoon vanilla extract

⅓ cup heavy whipping cream

3 tablespoons confectioner's sugar

⅓ cup mashed strawberries, fresh or thawed and drained

Directions

Line mini pie maker or muffin tins with bottom piecrusts for 4 pies. Press down to form indents, and cover with dried beans or pie weights to hold the crust in place. Bake in a mini pie maker for 4 to 6 minutes or in an oven preheated to 400 degrees for 8 to 12 minutes, or until crusts are crisp.

Remove crusts from pie maker or muffin tins and place on a large plate or baking tray.

Beat together the cream cheese, sugar, and vanilla. Stir in the mashed strawberries.

In a separate bowl, beat the cream until soft peaks form. Fold in the confectioner's sugar and then add to the cream cheese mixture. Stir to combine.

Spoon mixture into pre-baked shells and refrigerate for at least 2 hours before serving.

Coconut Cream Pies

Ingredients

Pastry for 4 bottom crusts

1 14-ounce can condensed milk

1 cup granulated sugar

2 tablespoons cornstarch

⅛ teaspoon salt

1 cup coconut flakes

Whipped cream, for serving

Directions

Line mini pie maker or muffin tins with bottom piecrusts for 4 pies. Press down to form indents, cover with dried beans or pie weights to hold the crust in place. Bake in a mini pie maker for 4 to 6 minutes or in an oven preheated to 400 degrees for 8 to 12 minutes, or until crusts are golden.

Remove crusts from pie maker or muffin tins and place on a large plate or baking tray.

Combine condensed milk, sugar, cornstarch, and salt in a saucepan and stir over low heat until mixture begins to thicken (about five to six minutes). Remove from heat and fold in coconut flakes. Divide filling between crusts and chill for about 2 hours before serving. Dollop whipped cream over each pie just before serving.

Dark Chocolate Cherry Pies

Ingredients

Chocolate pastry for 4 top and
  bottom crusts (see page 4)
2 cups pitted tart cherries (fresh or
  frozen)
2 tablespoons cornstarch

½ cup granulated sugar
⅛ teaspoon salt
1 teaspoon lemon juice
2 ounces dark chocolate, chopped
  in small pieces

Directions

Line mini pie maker or muffin tins with bottom piecrusts for 4 pies.

In a medium saucepan, cook the cherries with the cornstarch, sugar, salt, and lemon juice for about five minutes.

Divide filling between crusts. Sprinkle chocolate chunks over each pie.

Cover with top pastry rounds and bake in a mini pie maker for 8 to 10 minutes or in an oven preheated to 400 degrees for 12 to 15 minutes, or until the crusts are crisp.

Lemon Souffles

Ingredients

Pastry for 4 bottom crusts

2 tablespoons butter, softened

¾ cup sugar

2 eggs, separated

1½ tablespoons flour or cornstarch

1 lemon (juice and grated zest)

1½ cups evaporated milk

Whipped cream for serving

Directions

Line mini pie maker or muffin tins with bottom piecrusts for 4 pies.

Beat together the butter and sugar. Add the egg yolks, beating after each addition. Add flour or cornstarch, lemon juice, lemon zest, and condensed milk, and beat until combined.

In a separate bowl, beat egg whites until stiff. Fold lemon mixture into the egg whites.

Spoon filling into the crusts and bake in a mini pie maker for 8 to 10 minutes or in an oven preheated to 400 degrees for 12 to 15 minutes, or until the crusts are golden.

Serve with a dollop of whipped cream over each pie.

Orange Chocolate Pies

Ingredients

Chocolate pastry for 4 bottom crusts (see page 4)

6 ounces (¾ package) cream cheese, room temperature

3 tablespoons confectioners' sugar

1 8-ounce can sweetened condensed milk

¼ cup orange juice

⅓ cup heavy whipping cream

⅓ cup Mandarin orange slices, drained

½ cup semisweet chocolate chips

Directions

Line mini pie maker or muffin tins with bottom piecrusts for 4 pies. Press down to form indents, and cover with dried beans or pie weights to hold the crust in place. Bake in a mini pie maker for 4 to 6 minutes or in an oven preheated to 400 degrees for 8 to 12 minutes, or until crusts are golden.

Remove crusts from pie maker or muffin tins and place on a large plate or baking tray.

Beat together the cream cheese and sugar until fluffy. Add the sweetened condensed milk and orange juice and beat until smooth.

In a separate bowl, beat the cream until soft peaks form. Fold into the cream cheese mixture along with the Mandarin slices and chocolate chips.

Spoon mixture into pre-baked shells and refrigerate for at least two hours before serving.

Chocolate Raspberry Tarts

Ingredients

Pastry for 4 top and bottom crusts

1½ cups semisweet chocolate chips

⅛ teaspoon coarse salt

1 cup heavy cream

1 ½ cups fresh raspberries

Whipped cream, for serving

Directions

Line mini pie maker or muffin tins with bottom piecrusts for 4 pies. Press down to form indents, and cover with dried beans or pie weights to hold the crust in place. Bake in a mini pie maker for 4 to 6 minutes or in an oven preheated to 400 degrees for 8 to 12 minutes, or until crusts are golden.

Remove crusts from pie maker or muffin tins and place on a large plate or baking tray.

Place chocolate chips in a bowl. In a saucepan, heat heavy cream until it begins to simmer. Pour hot cream over the chocolate chips and stir until the mixture becomes smooth. Divide chocolate between tart shells. Chill for about half an hour.

Just before serving, arrange fresh raspberries over the chocolate filling in each pie and serve with whipped cream, if desired.

Iced Strawberry Mint Pies

Ingredients

Pastry for 4 bottom crusts

1 quart strawberry ice cream or
frozen yogurt, softened slightly

1 cup fresh strawberries, hulled and
sliced

2 tablespoons fresh mint, finely
chopped, plus a few leaves for
garnish

Directions

Line mini pie maker or muffin tins with bottom piecrusts for 4 pies. Press down to form indents, and cover with dried beans or pie weights to hold the crust in place. Bake in a mini pie maker for 4 to 6 minutes or in an oven preheated to 400 degrees for 8 to 12 minutes, or until crusts are golden.

Remove crusts from pie maker or muffin tins and place on a large plate or baking tray.

In a food processor, finely chop strawberries and mint. Fold into slightly softened frozen yogurt. Scoop into piecrusts and freeze for a couple hours before serving. Garnish with fresh mint leaves.

Lemon Ricotta Tarts with Ginger Cream

Ingredients

Pastry for 4 top and bottom crusts

1½ cups ricotta cheese

4 ounces (½ package) cream cheese, at room temperature

1 egg

⅓ cup granulated sugar

2 tablespoons grated lemon peel

2 tablespoons lemon juice

1 cup heavy or whipping cream

2 tablespoons honey

1 tablespoon finely chopped crystallized ginger

Directions

Line mini pie maker or muffin tins with bottom piecrusts for 4 pies.

Beat together the ricotta, cream cheese, egg, sugar, lemon peel, and lemon juice.

Divide filling between pies and bake in a mini pie maker for 12 to 14 minutes or in an oven preheated to 400 degrees 16 to 20 minutes or until filling is set.

To make the whipped cream, put cream in a bowl and beat until it begins to thicken. Drizzle honey in and continue to beat until soft peaks form. Fold in crystallized ginger bits just before serving.

Tollhouse Cookie Pies

Ingredients

Pastry for 4 top and bottom crusts

⅔ cup brown sugar

¼ cup all-purpose flour

2 eggs, lightly beaten

3 tablespoons butter, melted

1 teaspoon vanilla extract

1 cup peanuts, walnuts, or pecans, crushed

¾ cup chocolate chips

Directions

Line mini pie maker or muffin tins with bottom piecrusts for 4 pies.

Combine brown sugar, flour, eggs, butter, and vanilla. Add nuts and chocolate chips and mix.

Divide filling between crusts. Slice top pastry rounds into strips and form a lattice top over each pie. Bake in a mini pie maker for 8 to 10 minutes or in an oven preheated to 400 degrees for 12 to 15 minutes, or until crusts are golden and filling is set.

Peppermint Ice Cream Patty Pies

Ingredients

Pastry for 4 bottom crusts

1 quart peppermint ice cream or 1 quart vanilla ice cream mixed with 1 cup crushed candy canes, softened slightly at room temperature or in the microwave for about 20 seconds

12 chocolate sandwich cookies or 1 cup semisweet chocolate chips

Directions

Line mini pie maker or muffin tins with bottom piecrusts for 4 pies. Press down to form indents, and cover with dried beans or pie weights to hold the crust in place. Bake in a mini pie maker for 4 to 6 minutes or in an oven preheated to 400 degrees for 8 to 12 minutes, or until crusts are golden.

Remove crusts from pie maker or muffin tins and place on a large plate or baking tray.

Scoop softened ice cream into piecrusts. Decorate tops with sandwich cookies or chocolate chips. Freeze for about two before serving.

Banbury Tarts

Ingredients

Pastry for 4 bottom crusts
1 cup dried figs, chopped
½ cup raisins
1 egg
½ cup brown sugar

¼ cup walnuts
1 tablespoon brandy
1 tablespoon finely chopped orange peel

Directions

Place chopped figs and raisins in a heat-safe bowl and cover with boiling water. Allow to stand for 45 minutes, then drain.

Line mini pie maker or muffin tins with bottom piecrusts for 4 pies.

Beat together the egg and brown sugar. Add the brandy and mix. Add the drained figs and raisins, walnuts, and chopped orange peel.

Spoon filling into the piecrusts and bake in a mini pie maker for 8 to 10 minutes or in an oven preheated to 400 degrees for 12 to 15 minutes, or until crusts are golden and filling is set.

Pecan Cranberry Pies

Ingredients

Pastry for 4 bottom crusts

½ cup brown sugar

1 egg, lightly beaten

2 tablespoons maple syrup

1 cup pecans, halved

¼ cup dried cranberries

Directions

Line mini pie maker or muffin tins with bottom piecrusts for 4 pies.

Combine brown sugar, egg, and maple syrup. Add pecans and cranberries and mix.

Use a ladle to divide filling between crusts. Bake in a mini pie maker for 8 to 10 minutes or in an oven preheated to 400 degrees for 12 to 15 minutes, or until crusts are golden and filling is set.

Maple Walnut Pies

Ingredients

Pastry for 4 bottom crusts

½ cup brown sugar

1 egg, lightly beaten

2 tablespoons butter, melted

2 tablespoons maple syrup

1 teaspoon vanilla extract

1 cup walnuts, crushed

Directions

Line mini pie maker or muffin tins with bottom piecrusts for 4 pies.

Combine brown sugar, egg, butter, maple syrup, and vanilla. Add pecans and mix.

Use a ladle to divide filling between crusts. Bake in a mini pie maker for 8 to 10 minutes or in an oven preheated to 400 degrees for 12 to 15 minutes, or until crusts are golden and filling is set.

Choco-Nutty Bourbon Pies

Ingredients

Pastry for 4 top and bottom crusts

½ cup brown sugar

1 egg, lightly beaten

2 tablespoons butter, melted

2 tablespoons maple syrup or corn
 syrup

1 teaspoon vanilla extract

2 tablespoons bourbon

1 cup walnuts, crushed

⅔ cup chocolate chips

Directions

Line mini pie maker or muffin tins with bottom piecrusts for 4 pies.

Combine brown sugar, egg, butter, maple syrup or corn syrup, vanilla, and bourbon. Add walnuts and chocolate chips and mix.

Divide filling between crusts. Slice top pastry rounds into strips and form a lattice top over each pie. Bake in a mini pie maker for 8 to 10 minutes or in an oven preheated to 400 degrees for 12 to 15 minutes, or until crusts are golden.

Fresh Berry Mascarpone Tarts

Ingredients

Chocolate pastry for 4 bottom
 crusts (see page 4)
¾ cup mascarpone cheese
¼ cup Greek yogurt

3 tablespoons confectioner's sugar
½ teaspoon vanilla extract
2 cups fresh berries

Directions

Line mini pie maker or muffin tins with bottom piecrusts for 4 pies. Press down to form indents, and cover with dried beans or pie weights to hold the crust in place. Bake in a mini pie maker for 4 to 6 minutes or in an oven preheated to 400 degrees for 8 to 12 minutes, or until crusts are golden.

Remove crusts from pie maker or muffin tins and place on a large plate or baking tray.

Mix together the mascarpone cheese, Greek yogurt, confectioner's sugar, and vanilla extract. Just before serving, spoon the filling into the tart shells and top with fresh berries.

Toffee Almond Tarts

Ingredients

Pastry for 4 bottom crusts

1 cup heavy cream

¾ cup brown sugar

2 cups sliced almonds

¼ teaspoon almond extract

Directions

Line mini pie maker or muffin tins with bottom piecrusts for 4 pies.

In a medium saucepan, combine heavy cream and brown sugar. Bring to a boil and then reduce heat and simmer for about 5 minutes. Remove from heat and add almonds and almond extract. Use a ladle to divide filling between the shells.

Bake in a mini pie maker for 8 to 10 minutes or in an oven preheated to 400 degrees for 12 to 15 minutes, or until crusts are golden, filling is set, and tops of pies are caramelized.

Tea Time Lemon Tarts

Ingredients

Pastry for 4 bottom crusts

½ package (4 oz) cream cheese

¾ cup sugar

⅓ cup fresh lemon juice

2 teaspoons lemon zest

2 egg yolks, lightly beaten

½ cup milk

2 tablespoons cornstarch

2 tablespoons butter

½ cup sour cream

Whipped cream, for serving

Directions

Line mini pie maker or muffin tins with bottom piecrusts for 4 pies. Press down to form indents, and cover with dried beans or pie weights to hold the crust in place. Bake in a mini pie maker for 4 to 6 minutes or in an oven preheated to 400 degrees for 8 to 12 minutes, or until crusts are golden.

Remove crusts from pie maker or muffin tins and place on a large plate or baking tray.

In a medium saucepan, heat cream cheese, sugar, lemon juice, lemon zest, egg yolks, milk, and cornstarch. Stir regularly over medium heat and add butter. Cook until thickened, then remove from heat. Stir in sour cream. Refrigerate until ready to serve.

Just before serving, divide lemon filling between tart shells and top with whipped cream.

{ INDEX }

MY FAVORITE
MINI PIE RECIPES

_____

_____

_____

_____

_____

_____

_____

_____

_____

_____

_____

_____

_____

_____

_____

_____

_____

_____

_____

_____

_____

_____

CONVERSION CHARTS

METRIC AND IMPERIAL CONVERSIONS

(These conversions are rounded for convenience)

Ingredient	Cups/Tablespoons/ Teaspoons	Ounces	Grams/Milliliters
Butter	1 cup=16 tablespoons= 2 sticks	8 ounces	230 grams
Cream cheese	1 tablespoon	0.5 ounce	14.5 grams
Cheese, shredded	1 cup	4 ounces	110 grams
Cornstarch	1 tablespoon	0.3 ounce	8 grams
Flour, all-purpose	1 cup/1 tablespoon	4.5 ounces/0.3 ounce	125 grams/8 grams
Flour, whole wheat	1 cup	4 ounces	120 grams
Fruit, dried	1 cup	4 ounces	120 grams
Fruits or veggies, chopped	1 cup	5 to 7 ounces	145 to 200 grams
Fruits or veggies, pureed	1 cup	8.5 ounces	245 grams
Honey, maple syrup, or corn syrup	1 tablespoon	0.75 ounce	20 grams
Liquids: cream, milk, water, or juice	1 cup	8 fluid ounces	240 milliliters
Oats	1 cup	5.5 ounces	150 grams
Salt	1 teaspoon	0.2 ounces	6 grams
Spices: cinnamon, cloves, ginger, or nutmeg (ground)	1 teaspoon	0.2 ounce	5 milliliters
Sugar, brown, firmly packed	1 cup	7 ounces	200 grams
Sugar, white	1 cup/1 tablespoon	7 ounces/0.5 ounce	200 grams/12.5 grams
Vanilla extract	1 teaspoon	0.2 ounce	4 grams

The Magic of Mini Pies

OVEN TEMPERATURES

Fahrenheit	Celcius	Gas Mark
225°	110°	¼
250°	120°	½
275°	140°	1
300°	150°	2
325°	160°	3
350°	180°	4
375°	190°	5
400°	200°	6
425°	220°	7
450°	230°	8